HOPE FOR

ALL

MY GRIND TOWARDS GOD

DEREK BROWN

https://www.therealearthagatlin.com/

Hope For All: My Grind Toward God

© 2025

by

DEREK T. BROWN.

Cover design by Kate Wiliams.

Editor - Eartha Gatlin, Ahtrae Publishing, LLC

Book formatting by Kate Wiliams

All rights reserved.

Scripture quotations are taken from the Holy Bible TNIV

Author's note - Any reference to the 12 Steps of Alcoholics Anonymous are my reflections written in my own words and faith journey.

ISBNs: Print   979-8-218-81770-1

Ebook 979-8-218-81771-8

Library of Congress Cataloging in Publication Data

Name: Brown, Derek T., author

Description: Dallas, Texas Ahtrae Publishing, LLC, 2025

Identifiers: Library of Congress Control Number (LCCN) 2025921381

10 9 8 7 6 5 4 3 2 1

Printed in the United States of America

Published in the United States by Ahtrae Publishing, LLC

Dallas, Texas 2025

www.therealearthagatlin.com

DEDICATION

This book represents more than just a collection of pages; it embodies my journey, my struggles, and my triumphs. It is with immense gratitude that I dedicate this work to the remarkable women in my life who have unwaveringly believed in me, even during my darkest moments.

First, I would like to honor my mother, Susie Brown, whose boundless love and strength have been my guiding light. Her wisdom and resilience taught me the value of perseverance and compassion.

Next, I pay tribute to my sister, Shannon Brown, whose unbendable support and friendship have provided me with comfort and encouragement throughout my life. She has been my confidante, always ready to uplift me with her infectious spirit and laughter.

Most importantly, I want to express my deepest love and appreciation for my two beautiful daughters, Jasmine and D'Maia Brown. You are my pride and joy, and your innocent belief in me has given me the strength to keep pushing, even when I didn't think I could.

Lastly, I want to acknowledge my incredible wife, Cynequa Brown. Your patience and understanding have given me the freedom to grow and learn from my mistakes. I am profoundly thankful for your love, which has anchored me through life's challenges.

Thank you, ladies, for embracing me as I am and for granting me the time I needed to evolve. I cherish you all with every beat of my heart.

ACKNOWLEDGEMENTS

To all the wonderful people who saw hope in me during times when I struggled to see it in myself—thank you from the bottom of my heart. This book is a tribute to your unwavering support during my toughest times. When I hit rock bottom, caught in the grip of addiction, overwhelmed by despair, and teetering on the brink of a life that could end in tragedy or imprisonment, your presence was like a lifeline. You didn't let me give up. You stood by me, determined to help me fight against my circumstances. In moments when I felt too weak to carry on, you were my warriors, pushing me toward recovery with unyielding strength.

I am especially grateful to those who had the courage to share difficult truths with me when I desperately needed to hear them. Not to tear me down, but to wake me up and inspire me. Thank you to everyone who offered me second, third, or even more chances. Your kindness lit my way, showing me that redemption is real and found in extraordinary people like you.

You loved me through the chaos of my life. You reminded me that no matter how far I fell, there is always hope for healing. Most importantly, you never gave up on me, even when I succumbed to doubt and despair.

This book is dedicated to you. Each page captures the journey from just surviving to truly living, and it wouldn't exist without your incredible support.

Now, where do I begin? To everyone who helped me stand strong, kept me grounded, and refused to leave my side during my worst moments—thank you. You witnessed my struggles as I battled the weight of addiction and personal pain, yet you chose to believe in me. You encouraged me to fight for my life when giving up seemed so easy. You didn't sugarcoat the truth; you shared it honestly, exactly when I needed it. You reignited my desire to get back up and reclaim my life.

Your endless patience and kindness kept my spirit alive when I felt extinguished. The journey wasn't easy; I was stubborn, broken, angry, and lost. Yet, somehow, you loved me through every storm. You reminded me of my worth and the incredible potential within me, waiting to be brought to life.

This book isn't just a reflection of my journey. It's a shared story of our collective struggles and victories. I wouldn't be standing here today without you. I owe you more than words can express.

Thank you for believing in me, even when I couldn't believe in myself.

FOREWORD

Loving someone who's hurting is one of the hardest things you'll ever do. There were moments I felt helpless watching Derek lose himself to addiction, pain, and the lies he believed about who he was. I saw the light in him dimmed by the weight of his past and the choices he felt chained to. I prayed. I cried. I stayed quiet when my heart was screaming. And at times, I came close to breaking. Not because I didn't love him, but because I didn't know how much more I could watch him destroy himself.

But even in the darkest moments, I never stopped seeing the man I knew he could be. The man God created him to be. The man I always believed was still in there, buried under years of hurt, trauma, and survival.

Watching Derek rebuild himself has been one of the most powerful, humbling, and beautiful things I've ever experienced. I've seen him surrender to God. I've seen him face demons that nearly took him out. I've seen him grow into a loving father, a faithful husband, a true leader, and a man of deep conviction and purpose.

This book is his story. However, it's also a mirror for anyone who thinks they've gone too far or fallen too deep. Derek is proof that restoration is real. That no matter how far someone drifts, God's love can still reach them.

I'm proud of my husband. Not just because he changed, but because he fought for that change when it would've been easier to give up. He's walking in purpose now, and this book is a piece of that journey. I pray it brings hope to every soul that needs it.

Because I've seen firsthand: there is hope for all.

— Cynequa Brown

INTRODUCTION

REAL ONES ONLY

I ain't write this book to sound holy or polished. I wrote this because I know what it's like to be knee-deep in the mess, lost, drunk, mad at the world, and numb to everything. I know what it's like to stand on the corner, pockets empty, heart even emptier, wonderin' if life even got a point.

I come from the west side of Rockford. Where bullets talk louder than hope, where liquor flows easier than love, and where dreams don't just die, they get buried quick. I was raised in a place where pain was normal, where guns, gangs, and grief was everyday life. I didn't grow up in no safe space. I grew up dodgin' cops, runnin' from demons, and drownin' in bottles.

But somehow… God still had a plan.

This book ain't just about me. It's for that kid postin' up outside the gas station, wonderin' if his story even matters. It's for the man fightin' withdrawals, wonderin' if he can really change. It's for the ones cryin' in silence, screamin' for help nobody ever taught 'em how to ask for.

If you been hurt, I see you.

If you caught up in the bottle, I been there.

If you feel like hope packed up and left years ago—listen up.

God can pull you out the same gutter you crawled into. He can turn your lowest moment into your loudest testimony. I'm not preachin'. I'm speakin' from the trenches.

I know what it's like to wake up with vomit on your shirt and regret in your chest. I know how hard it is to say "no" when your whole body's screamin' for one more drink, one more escape. But I also know what it's like to hear your child laugh and know they're laughin' with you, not at you. That's real redemption. That's God. This book ain't about bein' perfect. It's about gettin' free.

So, if you ever grew up without a father…

If you lost homies to the streets or drugs…

If you thought your zip code was your sentence…

If you ever looked in the mirror and didn't recognize who you saw…

This is for you.

You're not too far gone.

You're not beyond savin'.

You still got purpose.

I ain't no hero. I'm just proof that God can work with a mess and still create a masterpiece. I made it out. And now I'm reachin' back to show you—you can too.

TABLE OF CONTENTS

REAL ONES ONLY

PART 1

THE STRUGGLE

BORN INTO BROKENNESS

PART 2

THE BREAKIN' POINT

PART 3

THE RISE

PART 4

THE MISSION

HOPE FOR

ALL

MY GRIND TOWARDS
GOD

DEREK BROWN

PART 1

THE STRUGGLE

CHAPTER 1

BORN INTO BROKENNESS

West side of Rockford wasn't no school with desks and teachers. It was the block that raised me. Concrete jungle. Ain't no family dinners or bedtime stories over here—just cold nights, loud fights, and sirens singin' us to sleep. The sidewalks were cracked like our homes, liquor stores posted up on every corner like they was part of the neighborhood crew. Neon lights glowed like they had answers, but all they gave was another escape route that led straight to hell.

I wasn't born into love. I was born into survival mode. From day one, it was hustle or starve. We didn't talk about poverty—we lived it. Empty fridges. Lights cut off. Mama tryin' to stretch a dollar like it was magic. Christmas? Man, that just reminded us what we ain't have. While other kids were unwrappin' presents, I was unwrappin' pain and disappointment. Childhood wasn't no fairy tale. It was war—and I was drafted early.

Gangs were already outside before I even knew what the word meant. I used to peep the older dudes posted up, iced out, stackin' bread, movin' with that swagger. They had the streets on lock. I thought that was power.

I thought that was success. I ain't realize that behind all that flash was a fast road to nowhere: jail, death, or both. But when you ain't got no other example, that street life starts lookin' like the only option.

I ain't have a pops around to steer me right. My moms? She was out here fightin' her own battles, tryin' to hold it down the best she could. I saw her grind. I saw her break. I saw her get back up. But even a strong mama can't fill the hole left by a missin' father. Most of the dudes I knew were either gone, locked up, or so numb from their own trauma that they might as well had not been there at all.

See, when you grow up in a spot like this, the streets try to script your future for you. They tell you, "You gon' be just like the rest—angry, addicted, dead, or in the system." And if you ain't got someone to tell you otherwise, you start believin' it. You start wearin' that pain like armor, thinkin' love is soft and dreams are for fools.

But deep down… I still had a spark. I ain't know what it was or where it came from, but I felt it. Like maybe—just maybe—I was meant for more than just the west side of Rockford. More than these cold streets. More than the bottle. More than the violence.

I was just a lost kid, tryna figure out how to live in a world that never taught me how.

CHAPTER 2

ESCAPIN' REALITY

When life start swingin' on you with no breaks, storm after storm, it's only a matter of time before you look for somethin' to take the edge off. For me, that "somethin" was alcohol. That bottle became my best friend and my worst enemy.

I ain't drink to party. I wasn't tryna turn up or chase no good time. I drank to forget. To numb the noise in my head. To silence the screams from back home. The yellin', the gunshots, the sound of my mama cryin' in the next room thinkin' I couldn't hear. That pain? It was loud. And liquor? That was the mute button on the noise in my head.

My pops? Ghost. He wasn't around to teach me what being a man even meant. So, I made it up as I went. Watched the streets. Copied the wrong dudes. And deep down, I could see the hurt in my mama's eyes. She was holdin' the whole house on her back, but I was too wrapped up in my own pain to step up.

The first time I got drunk, man…it was like I floated away. No pain. No fear. Just… silence. For once, I ain't feel broken. I ain't feel like that scared little kid from the West

Side. But that feelin'? It ain't last. And the more I chased it, the more it ran from me.

Pretty soon, the bottle wasn't just a "sometimes" thing. It was every day. Wake up, drink. Hurt, drink. Breathe, drink. School didn't matter. Goals didn't matter. I started hangin' with older cats who looked like they had it all. The money, girls, respect. But they was just like me broken. They just dressed their wounds in designer clothes and dope cars.

I was searchin' for somethin'. Some love, an identity, a purpose, but I looked for it in all the wrong places. I thought drinkin' made me grown. Thought actin' tough made me a man. Truth is, I was scared out my mind. I didn't know who I was. Every sip just pushed me further from the truth.

On the outside, I played the role. I was cool, collected, in control. But inside? I was fallin' apart. People saw a man, but I was still that little boy just wantin' somebody, anybody to see I was drownin'.

Addiction talks slick. It tells you, "This is it for you. You ain't never gon' be more than this." And after a while, I started to believe that lie. Started thinkin' the bottle was the only thing that understood me.

But somewhere in that chaos, I swear there was a flicker. A whisper. A tug. God was there. Even when I was wildin' out. Even when I was numb and runnin' from everything real. I ain't see it back then, but now I know He never left.

Lookin' back, I see the drinkin' for what it really was. It wasn't just a habit. It was a warning. My soul was cryin' for help, but all I gave it was another shot. Another excuse. Another lie that I was still in control.

Addiction don't care about you. It wants your peace, your purpose, your family, your life. It eats and eats until you got nothin' left but regrets and hangovers.

I ain't know it yet, but I was speedin' toward a dead end. Everything that mattered was hangin' by a thread. And the liquor? It wasn't savin' me. It was slowly killin' me.

But even in that darkness...God wasn't done with me yet.

CHAPTER 3

CHAINED BUT NOT LOST

Addiction feels like bein' locked up in a cell with no bars. You walk around lookin' normal, smilin' in pictures, crackin' jokes, goin' to work like you got it all together. But deep down? You're shackled. Tied up in chains nobody else can see. And the worst part? Most people don't even notice. They don't ask, and even if they did, you wouldn't know how to explain the weight you carry every day.

I can't even count how many times I told myself and the people I love "I'm done." I meant it every single time. I wasn't tryna lie. I really thought I could stop. But then somethin' small would hit like stress at work, drama at home, feelin' alone. Then next thing I know, I'm right back at the liquor store, makin' that same tired excuse: "Just one."

I wish I was just drinkin' as a social thing. Kickin' it with the homies, celebratin', forgettin' the pain for a while. But it was somethin' else. I wasn't drinkin' to vibe.. I was drinkin' to survive. I didn't even want to get drunk sometimes. I just didn't know how to live sober. The bottle wasn't just a habit. It became part of my identity. Livin' without it felt like losin' a part of who I was.

That's when I realized I wasn't in control anymore. I was in chains. And I didn't even know where the key was. The more I drank, the more damage I caused. People started fallin' back. They stopped callin'. They stopped trustin'. They got tired of the lies, the broken promises, the missed birthdays, the empty apologies. I don't blame 'em. I was unreliable. I was selfish. I was so deep in my addiction, I couldn't see how much I was hurtin' the ones who actually cared.

I started missin' out on life. Moments passed me by like cars on the freeway—fast, blurry, gone. I'd wake up not knowin' how I got home. Look in the mirror and barely recognize the dude starin' back. Sometimes I'd wonder if that was the night I almost died. Sometimes I wouldn't care if I did.

But through all of it, even at my lowest, I swear God had His hand on me. Not 'cause I earned it. Not 'cause I was worthy. But 'cause

He had a plan. Even when I was deep in the mess, He was already movin' behind the scenes. Workin' on my rescue before I even asked for help.

There was one night that hit different. Everything was quiet. No distractions. Just me, a bottle, and my thoughts. I had pushed everybody away. My room was dim, my spirit even darker. I sat there thinkin', "Is this it? Is this how my story ends?" I wasn't tryna take my life, but I wasn't exactly tryna live either. That kinda hopelessness? It's dangerous.

Then, outta nowhere, this small voice hit me, *"This ain't who you are."*

It was like somethin' cracked inside me. A little burn. But sometimes, that's all it takes. That one moment gave me a reason to try. It didn't fix everything overnight, but it reminded me that I wasn't too far gone.

I want you to hear me when I say this:

Just 'cause you in chains don't mean you forgotten. Just 'cause you strugglin' don't mean you worthless. And just 'cause you lost don't mean you can't be found.

I was beat down, ashamed, and afraid. But even in all that mess, I knew I wasn't alone. God never turned His back on me. He saw past the addiction, past the pain, past the broken pieces, and He still believed in the man I could be.

Even before I had the strength to fight back, He was already layin' the path for my comeback.

I wasn't free yet...but I wasn't fightin' alone no more.

PART 2

THE BREAKIN' POINT

CHAPTER 4

WHEN ENOUGH WAS
ENOUGH

Every comeback story got that one moment where the pain gets too heavy, the lies catch up, and you finally stop runnin' from the truth. For me, it didn't happen in no church pew or up on some quiet mountaintop. Nah. My moment came on a dirty floor, in a dark room, surrounded by concrete walls and the wreckage of my own life.

That night, I hit rock bottom.

It wasn't one big crash. It was years of slow motion fallin', messin' up, losin' trust, pushin' people away, and killin' myself from the inside out. But this night? It broke me. For real. I was laid out on a cold-ass floor at Winnebago County Jail, I kept losin'. The air smelled like pain and old liquor. The silence? Loud. My life? A damn mess.

No pride left.

No strength left.

No more excuses.

I was done blamin' my past. Done frontin' like I had it under control. I'd tried to clean my act up time and time again. I'd tell myself, "This time's different." But every time, I'd fall right back into the same cycle. Nothin' ever stuck. Nothin' ever healed what was really goin' on inside.

That night I ain't feel lost. I felt empty. Hollow. Like a shell of who I used to be. Then outta nowhere, I broke down in tears. Real ones. The kind that don't stop once they start. I couldn't hold it in no more.

And in that broken moment, I whispered the realest prayer I ever prayed, *"God, if You real... help me. Please."*

It wasn't fancy. It wasn't churchy. It was just me, broken, beat up, and tired, beggin' for help.

And I believe He heard me.

I didn't get struck by lightnin'. The roof ain't open up. But somethin' shifted. I felt the weight of all that frontin' lift off my chest. For the first time in years, I felt a flicker of somethin'...hope.

I ain't wake up the next mornin' a new man. My problems didn't vanish. But that night taught me two things that changed my life:

I couldn't do this alone.

And I didn't have to.

That was the beginnin' of my surrender. Not just to sobriety, but to God. I stopped tryin' to be my own savior. I stopped actin' like I had it all together. That night, I finally admitted: "*I need Jesus.*"

This wasn't just about quittin' the bottle. It was about layin' everything down. My control. My pride. My past. I put it all in God's hands. And in return? He gave me somethin' I hadn't felt in a long time... peace. A little hope. A little light.

So, if you readin' this and you feel like you at your end, listen to me:

You ain't too far gone.

You ain't too broken.

And you definitely ain't alone.

God still hears broken people cryin' out in dark places. He still shows up in messy rooms with empty bottles and heavy hearts. And He still turns rock bottoms into fresh starts. That night wasn't my end. It was the night I decided to fight for my life.

CHAPTER 5

STEPS TOWARDS SOBRIETY

Sobriety don't come with balloons and celebration cakes. Nah. It comes in silence. It comes with fear. It comes with your hands shakin', your mind racin', and your soul beggin' for peace.

The mornin' after I cried out to God? That joint felt unreal. My head was poundin', my stomach twisted up, and the room was dead quiet. The bottles were gone. The noise? Gone. The chaos I used to live in? Gone. And for the first time in a long time, it was just me. No distractions. Just me and the aftermath of all the choices I made.

But deep in that silence, I felt somethin' different. It was small but it was real. I ain't know what tomorrow was gon' look like. I couldn't even think about the next 30 days. All I knew was I had to survive the next 30 minutes without pickin' up a bottle.

THE FIRST 30 DAYS

People who ain't been through it won't ever understand what detox feels like. It's war. Your body wildin' out, sweatin', shakin', fiendin'. Your brain goin' a hundred miles an hour, and your emotions swingin' like fists in a street fight.

Some days I was angry at the world. Other days I couldn't get outta bed. Sometimes I'd just start cryin' for no reason and with no warnin'. Just pain leakin' out my eyes.

But I made one solid choice:

I wasn't goin' back to the bottle.

That choice forced me to flip everything upside down. I had to check my whole life. Check where I was hangin', who I was kickin' it with, what I was listenin' to, even what I was lettin' sit in my mind. See, the bottle wasn't the root; it was just the band-aid I'd been slappin' on top of deep pain, trauma, and lies I carried for years.

So, I had to fill that empty space with somethin' new. Somethin' real.

I started readin' Scripture even when I didn't understand it. I posted verses on my mirror with sticky notes, 'cause I needed that truth in my face every single day. I prayed.

Even if all I could say was "God, help me." That was enough.

ONE DAY AT A TIME

I ain't set out thinkin' I'd be four years sober. That would've crushed me. All I wanted was to make it through today.

That mindset? That saved me. If I looked too far ahead, I'd panic. If I stared too long at the past, I'd drown in regret. But if I stayed in the moment, just right now, I had a shot.

Each night I made it without drinkin', I whispered, "Thank You, God."

Not 'cause I was strong, but 'cause He was holdin' me up.

Sobriety ain't about willpower. it's about Jesus. Every day, I had to choose to feel what I used to numb. I had to sit with the guilt, the shame, the fear, and let God start healin' what I'd been runnin' from for years.

THE POWER OF ACCOUNTABILITY

Here's the real: You can't do this alone.

I had to get honest with a few solid brothers I could trust. Dudes I could hit up and say, "Yo, I'm strugglin' today," and they wouldn't judge me or feed me some weak advice. They'd pray with me. Remind me who I was. Remind me Who I belonged to.

At the same time, I had to cut some people off. Not 'cause I didn't love 'em, but because I couldn't keep sittin' in the same mud expectin' to stay clean. You can't walk forward when you still hangin' with what's tryin' to pull you back.

Temptation still came. It always does. But I had people to call. I had prayers to lean on. I had truth to stand on.

A NEW KIND OF STRENGTH

People think strength means holdin' it all together. But I learned real strength is about lettin' go.

I had to lay it all down—my pride, my pain, my past. Every day I gave it to the One who created me. The One who never gave up on me. The One who kept me alive when I should've been dead.

That's how I stayed sober. That's how I stay sober. Not by tryin' harder. But by stayin' closer to God, to the truth, and to the people who love me enough to keep it real.

PART 3

THE RISE

CHAPTER 6

BUILDIN' A NEW MAN

Sobriety wasn't the finish line. It was just the beginnin'. When the fog started clearin' from all the alcohol and chaos, I had one loud question hittin' me like a brick: *"What now?"*

See, for years I was just tryna stay alive. Duckin' pain, drownin' trauma, livin' minute to minute. I didn't know how to live; I only knew how to survive. I ain't have a clue how to show up on time, how to pay bills on time, or how to sit with my emotions without tryin' to numb 'em.

I had to rebuild. From scratch. From the ground up. No shortcuts. No street game. Just real growth, step by step. And the first real lesson I had to learn? You can't build a new life while holdin' on to old habits.

WORK: CHANGIN' MY GRIND

Back then, "work" meant hustle—fast money, dirty money, street money. I thought as long as I had a few bills in my pocket, I was good. But all I was doin' was stayin' stuck. That grind didn't build nothin' but pain, paranoia, and prison time for people like me.

So, I humbled myself. I took jobs nobody was braggin' about. Entry-level stuff. No glamor. No spotlight. Just honest work. I showed up early, stayed late, and gave it everything I had even when I ain't feel like it. And guess what? That grind started changin' me. It wasn't just about the paycheck. It was about the discipline. The responsibility. The dignity. I was finally doin' somethin' I could be proud of—somethin' that didn't come with guilt or regret.

I built a daily routine: wake up early, knock out tasks, pray, read, reflect. I didn't need chaos no more. I was learnin' how to build peace. One borin', faithful step at a time.

FINDIN' STABILITY

Where I came from, stability felt weird. The streets always moved fast. Drama was everywhere. And if it was quiet? You knew somethin' was about to go down. But now? I started wantin' peace more than I wanted excitement. I made structure part of my life. Same wake-up time. Same bedtime. I prayed in the mornin'. I made a budget. I started eatin' at the table instead of off the couch. Real basic stuff. But man, that basic became powerful. I used to think routine was borin'. But what's really borin' is watchin' your life fall apart over and over again. What's really exhaustin' is chasin' highs that always leave you empty. Buildin' somethin' solid? That gave me real joy.

PROTECTIN' MY CIRCLE

One of the hardest things I had to do was distance myself from certain people. Not 'cause I didn't love 'em, but because I was tryna live, and they were comfortable dyin'. Some folks liked the broken version of me. They liked the drunk me. The messy me. 'Cause it made them feel better about where they were. But once I started changin', it got quiet.

Some of 'em ghosted me. Others tried to pull me back in. So, I made a decision: I gotta protect my peace like my life depends on it— 'cause it does. I started surroundin' myself with real ones. Brothers who challenged me. Mentors who told me the truth, even when it stung. Friends who showed up without askin' for anything in return. People who prayed with me, checked me, and helped me grow. I learned quick: You can't grow if your circle's stuck. You want to be better? Then be around better.

LOOKIN' BACK TO MOVE FORWARD

Where I'm at today ain't luck. It's grace and hard work. Yeah, God saved me. No doubt. But I had to show up every day and do my part. I was given a second chance, but it was on me to make it count. I had to let go of the old me to become the man I was always meant to be. Not perfect. Not polished. But real. Redeemed. Focused.

Brick by brick, I started buildin' a new man. And this time? I ain't doin' it alone.

CHAPTER 7

BECOMIN' A FAMILY MAN

I ain't grow up in no picture-perfect family. There wasn't no bedtime stories, no 'I love yous,' no safe place to cry. It was straight up survival. We weren't buildin' memories; we were just tryin' to make it to the next day without breakin' apart.

Love didn't live in that house. Fear did. Anger did. Bills piled up, emotions stayed bottled up, and everything felt like a fight— sometimes with the world, sometimes with each other.

So, when I started this healin' journey, one prayer stayed on my heart: *"Lord, help me become the man I never had."* I wasn't just askin' to be better. I was askin' to break a generational curse. I didn't have no blueprint for what it meant to be a husband or a father, so I had to build mine from scratch. I had to unlearn what pain taught me and relearn what love was supposed to look like.

UNPACKIN' THE BAGGAGE

Before I could lead a family, I had to face myself. I was carryin' scars from my childhood into every relationship. I didn't even know I was doin' it. That pride? That distance? That fear of messin' everything up?

All that came from the wounds I never dealt with. I started the real work. I had to forgive my father for disappearin'. I had to forgive myself for the hurt I caused. I had to stop runnin' from hard convos and start speakin' truth with love. I learned that bein' emotionally present ain't weak; it's brave. It means not walkin' out when things get uncomfortable. It means listenin' even when my ego tells me to defend myself. And it means showin' love through action, not just words.

REDEFININ' FATHERHOOD

The first time my kid called me "Daddy," man, I almost broke down. Not 'cause I was sad, but because it healed a piece of me I didn't even know was still cracked. Bein' a father ain't about just throwin' money on the table. It's about showin' up every single day. It's bedtime stories. It's prayers at the dinner table. It's bein' there when they're scared, hypin' 'em up when they win, and correctin' 'em with love when they slip. I wanted my kids to see a different kind of man. One who don't run when things get tough. One who treats their mama with love and respect, even when it's hard. 'Cause how I treat her teaches my stepsons how to be men and shows my daughters what kind of love they should accept. I wanted to build a home—not just a house. A place where they felt safe. A place where peace lived, not just four walls and a roof.

BEIN' A REAL HUSBAND

Bein' a husband ain't about control. It ain't about bein' right. It's about servin' your family with love and humility. I had to learn to say, "I'm sorry." I had to learn to forgive, even when I was hurt. I had to learn to lead by followin' Jesus first. I started prayin' over my wife and kids. I got back into the Word, not just to quote it, but to live it. I made it a point to fill our home with somethin' I never had growin' up—peace, love, and God's presence. Some days I still felt like that same broken kid from the West Side. But I kept showin' up anyway because that's what real men do.

BREAKIN' THE CYCLE

I ain't had the best role model. But now? I am the role model. And if you're anything like me, if you came from a place where love was hard to find, you don't have to repeat that cycle. You can choose different. You can raise your kids with purpose. You can love your woman with honor. You can build a home filled with joy, truth, and grace.

You ain't disqualified because of your past. You're qualified by the way you fight for your future. Every day, I'm still learnin'.

Still growin'. Still leanin' on God. But one thing I know for sure: I'm not who I used to be. And by God's grace, my kids won't have to heal from the same stuff I did.

CHAPTER 8

FINDIN' JESUS IN
ROCKFORD

Most folks think you gotta go somewhere quiet like some retreat in the woods or a church up on a hill to find God. Like peace only lives in calm places. But for me?

I found Jesus right in the middle of the mess. Right there on the west side of Rockford. Right there in the same streets that almost took me out. The same blocks I used to run wild on… that's where I met my Savior.

Jesus didn't wait for me to clean up or get my act together. He stepped into the middle of my chaos and said, *"I'm here. I never left. And I still want you."*

A SAVIOR IN THE CHAOS

For a long time, I thought Jesus was just for church folks. You know the ones. People in suits, speakin' proper, passin' judgment, and pretendin' they had it all together. I didn't think He had anything to do with someone like me. Not someone broken. Not someone addicted. Not someone angry at the world.

But I was wrong. Jesus wasn't sittin' up in some fancy church with a gavel in His hand. He was with me in the gutter. He was with me in the back room, in the drunk nights, in the moments where I wanted to give up. He wasn't shoutin' rules at me. He was whisperin', *"You were made for more than this."*

It wasn't therapy, money, or rehab that saved me. It was grace. That real, undeserved, heavy-hittin', soul-shakin' grace that only comes from Jesus Christ. I picked up a Bible one day, not even sure what I was lookin' for... and it felt like the pages were readin' me. It didn't feel fake. It felt honest. Like it was talkin' to the pain I had buried so deep.

Then I read this:

"Therefore, if anyone is in Christ, he is a new creation; old things have passed away, and look, new things have come."

(2 Corinthians 5:17)

That hit me in my chest. I didn't wanna just change. I wanted to be reborn.

CHURCH AIN'T ABOUT A BUILDIN'

I didn't find Jesus in a mega-church with light shows and stadium seatin'. I found Him in a raggedy room—foldin' chairs, cheap coffee, and real people who had been through hell like me. Nobody pretended. Nobody judged. People cried durin' worship. They prayed hard. They hugged without hesitation. And when I walked in feelin' like I didn't belong, they looked me dead in the eye and said, "We're glad you're here."

That was church. Not a performance. Not a social club. But a hospital for the broken. I didn't need religion. I needed relationship. I needed brothers who would pray for me, not laugh at me. I needed accountability that wasn't fake. I needed worship to replace wild nights. I needed Scripture to be louder than the lies I kept tellin' myself.

JESUS GAVE ME A NEW IDENTITY

When I gave my heart to Jesus, I didn't just get forgiveness. I got purpose. I stopped walkin' around carryin' names like "addict," "failure," "loser," or "lost cause." Now I walk with a new name: Son of God. I ain't who I used to be. I'm not that drunk dude crashin' on couches. I'm not that angry man pushin' everyone away. I'm not that broken kid from Rockford who thought he'd never be nothin'. I'm a new creation. Not because I fixed myself, but because Jesus did what I couldn't. Faith didn't just clean me up. It defined me.

Now, I wake up every day choosin' Jesus. Not just on Sundays. Not just when I'm down bad. Every day. I stay in the Word 'cause I need His voice louder than my own doubts. I pray 'cause I know I ain't strong enough on my own. I worship not 'cause I'm holy, but 'cause I remember where I came from… and I never wanna go back.

IF HE CAN SAVE ME

If you think Jesus ain't for you 'cause you been through too much…If you think your record, your mistakes, your past disqualify you…You're wrong. He saw all of it and still went to the cross for you. He saw your worst nights and said, "I still want you."

If He could find me in Rockford, in the middle of addiction, shame, and failure then He can find you wherever you're at. Don't wait till you're "cleaned up." Don't wait for some perfect moment. Come as you are. Right now. He's already waitin'. Arms wide open. Just like He was for me.

PART 4

THE MISSION

CHAPTER 9

REACHIN' BACK WHILE MOVIN' FORWARD

Getting' out of that life? That was just the start. The real work came when I realized I couldn't just run from my past. I had to go back and pull somebody else out with me.

There's a moment, after the noise fades, when God whispers, "It' s time." Time to stop just survivin' and start givin' back. Not to relive the pain, but to be the hand somebody else grabs when they're about to fall.

BECOMIN' THE SUPPORT I NEEDED

I didn't grow up with a real man tellin' me, "You can be better than this." No one said, "Your story ain 't over." I had to figure that out for myself. Now, I'm that voice for young men still stuck where I was. I ain't there preachin' or judgin'. I'm there talkin', listenin', sharin' my story like it's theirs too. Because it is. We all got scars. We all got battles. And sometimes, what folks need most is someone who's been through it and still made it out.

Some of these young men I talk to have already lost friends to gunfire. Others got records that feel like chains around their necks. Some are fathers who don't know their kids. I get it, because I walked that road too.

MENTORSHIP OVER PREACHIN'

The streets don't want another voice tellin' them what to do. They want someone who's been through the fire and came out real. Someone who doesn't pretend. Someone who shows up.

I'm not here to fix 'em. I'm here to walk with them through the struggle, through the doubt, through the mess. Whether it's drivin' a brother to his first recovery meetin', helpin' him write a résumé, or just bein' there when the night gets too dark, I'm present.

It's about bein' consistent, not perfect. It's about showin' up, not standin' on stages.

PLANTIN' SEEDS IN TOUGH SOIL

Sometimes it hurts when I see someone slip back. When words fall on deaf ears.

When folks drift away. But this ain't about instant results. This is about plantin' seeds. Seeds of hope, truth, and love.

Some seeds grow quick. Some take their time. And some may never sprout. But I'll keep plantin' because someone once did that for me.

MOVIN' FORWARD WITHOUT FORGETTIN'

I'm growin' into a better husband, father, worker, and man of faith. But I carry my past like a badge, not a chain. I don't go back to prove somethin'. I go back 'cause love doesn't forget where it came from.

If you've found your way out, don't just walk away from your story. Step back in with purpose. Reach out. Mentor a lost brother. Share your hard-won hope. Be the light in someone's dark.

There's someone out there who needs to hear: "You ain't gotta give up. There's a better way. And I'll help you find it." If God can use my broken past to build somethin' new, He can do the same for you.

CHAPTER 10

A NEW LEGACY

People hear the word "legacy" and start thinkin' about money, trust funds, big houses, shiny cars, stacks in the bank. That's cool and all, but real legacy ain't about what you leave for people… it's about what you leave in them. It's about how your kids remember you. It's about the pain they don't have to carry. It's about breakin' the cycle so the next generation ain't stuck in the same storm you fought your way out of.

For a long time, I didn't think I had a choice. I thought I had to carry what my daddy carried. I thought I was just another broken man from a broken family, and that's all I'd ever be. But when I gave my life to Jesus, I realized somethin' crazy powerful: I don't have to pass that pain down anymore. I can build somethin' different. Somethin' better.

FLIPPIN' THE SCRIPT

My family came up hard—no fathers in the house, addiction runnin' wild, too many wounds and not enough healin'. The pain got passed down like an old jacket that never fit right. But I decided: That cycle ends with me.

My kids ain't gonna grow up wonderin' if Daddy loves them. They ain't gonna hear me yellin' through walls or see me passed out on the couch with a bottle in my hand. They're gonna see me prayin' over them, showin' up for their games, lovin' their mama, and leadin' our home with strength and grace. I want them to grow up knowin' they matter. That they were created on purpose, for a purpose. I want them to hear me say, *"You are loved. You are seen. And you're never alone."*

And listen, I know my kids will have their own struggles—but they won't be stuck fighting the demons I left behind. That's the legacy I'm leavin' them.

If you think it's too late for you, I'm tellin' you right now: It's not. God can flip your whole life. You just gotta give Him the pen and let Him rewrite the story.

FROM SURVIVAL TO PURPOSE

I used to wake up just tryna get through the day. Now, I wake up askin' *"How can I serve? Who can I bless?, What part of my story can help someone else today?"*

God didn't pull me out the fire just so I could sit in comfort. He rescued me to redeploy me. To turn my wounds into wisdom. My pain into purpose.

Every hard night, every ugly cry, every setback and slip-up, none of it was wasted. God is usin' all of it. Now I walk through the same neighborhoods that almost killed me. But now I do it with a new kind of swagger; not to flex, but to give hope. I ain't perfect, but I'm proof that change is real.

LEGACY TAKES WORK

Don't get it twisted. This journey still takes work. I still get tempted. I still get tired.

But I don't fight alone anymore. I stay locked in by:

- Stayin' in the Word, 'cause God's truth drowns out the lies I used to believe.
- Prayin' daily, even if all I can say some days is "Lord, help me."
- Leanin' on my circle, because healin' happens in community, not isolation.
- Livin' with purpose, not just vibes. I move based on conviction, not feelin's.

Some days feel slow. Some feel heavy. But I keep showin' up. Because every day I stay faithful, I'm stackin' bricks on somethin' that'll outlive me. I'm buildin' a home where peace lives. I'm buildin' a name my kids can carry with pride. I'm buildin' a story that shows others: you can come back from anything.

YOU CAN CHANGE THE NARRATIVE

You might be readin' this thinkin', "Man, I've already messed it up too much."

Nah, not true. Jesus is still writin'. You're still breathin'. And as long as there's breath in your lungs, there's still hope. Your past doesn't disqualify you. It equips you. God's not lookin' for perfect people. He's lookin' for willin' ones.

You can leave behind a new kind of legacy: One filled with healin', not trauma. Faith, not fear. Love, not shame.

It starts with one decision: Give it all to Jesus. Every mistake, every scar, every regret. And then… don't look back. Let your kids, your community, and everyone around you see what redemption looks like with skin on. Let them see the new legacy you're livin'.

APPENDIX

DAILY PRAYERS, SCRIPTURES, AND REAL TALK FOR THE JOURNEY

This journey is about more than just staying sober; it's about living each day with purpose and intention. Whether you're just starting to overcome addiction or have been on your healing path for years, this collection of prayers, verses, and reflection tools is here to help you stay focused, uplift your spirits, and clarify your goals.

MORNING PRAYER

"Lord, as I wake up today, I dedicate this day to You. Help me stay grounded, stay sober, and be true to myself. Guide me so I don 't fall back into the chaos I've escaped. I' m grateful for the gift of today and for the purpose it brings. Help me face whatever challenges come my way. In Jesus' name, Amen."

EVENING PRAYER

"God, I thank You for giving me the strength to get through another day. Even if today wasn't perfect, being here shows that You have a plan for me. Please forgive my mistakes and help me learn from them. Grant me a peaceful night' s sleep and the strength

I need for tomorrow. In Jesus' name, Amen."

VERSES FOR STRENGTH AND ENCOURAGEMENT

1. "When someone is in Christ, they are a new person; the old is gone, and the new has come!" (2 Corinthians 5:17)

   - This verse reminds us that our past does not define who we are.

2. "The Lord is close to the brokenhearted; He saves those who are crushed in spirit." (Psalm 34:18)

- Even in our toughest moments, God is there to comfort us.

3. "Don't let the world around you change you, but let God change the way you think…" (Romans 12:2)

- Real change starts from within as we work toward a hopeful and purposeful life.

4. "He who began a good work in you will carry it on until it is completed." (Philippians 1:6)

- This is a reminder that God continues to work in us.

5. "I am doing something new; do you not see it?" (Isaiah 43:19)

- Even if we can't see the changes, God is working to renew our lives.

QUESTIONS FOR REFLECTION

Use these questions to think deeply, record your growth, or start discussions with friends or mentors:

PART 1: THE STRUGGLE

1. What untrue beliefs did your tough experiences teach you about yourself?

_____

_____

_____

2. How did your struggles lead you to a point where you felt broken?

_____

_____

_____

3. Is there someone you need to forgive to truly heal and move forward?

_____

_____

_____

PART 2: THE BREAKING POINT

1. What moment made you say, "I can't keep living like this"?

   _____

   _____

   _____

2. Can you remember the most heartfelt prayer you said when you reached out to God?

   _____

   _____

   _____

3. What pain are you holding onto that you need to let go of to move forward?

   _____

   _____

   _____

PART 3: THE RISE

1.What positive habits are you building to replace the harmful ones?

_____

_____

_____

2.How can you see God helping you become more disciplined in your everyday life?

_____

_____

_____

3.In what ways can you take on leadership roles to inspire others around you?

_____

_____

_____

PART 4: THE MISSION

1. Who in your life could benefit from the lessons and hope you've gained?

_____

_____

_____

2. How do you feel about "legacy" now that you're trying to live with purpose?

_____

_____

_____

3. How do you want your children, nieces, nephews, or community to remember you in the future?

_____

_____

_____

RESOURCES FOR RECOVERY & REBUILDING

To support you in your recovery, consider these helpful resources:

FAITH-BASED RECOVERY PROGRAMS

- Celebrate Recovery

  A program focused on healing through faith.
- The Most Excellent Way:

  A community aimed at personal growth and spiritual healing.
- Teen Challenge / Adult & Teen Challenge

  Long-term programs that offer guidance and support for recovery.

COUNSELING & THERAPY OPTIONS

- Look for Christian counseling centers often linked to local churches.
- Check out affordable clinics that offer sliding-scale fees in your community.
- Join support groups for trauma and grief to understand more about healing.

ACCOUNTABILITY & MENTORSHIP OPPORTUNITIES

- Participate in men's or women's groups at your church.
- Get involved in one-on-one mentorship programs for personal growth.
- Find a mentor who has experience in overcoming similar challenges and is willing to share advice.

JOB & LIFE SKILLS SUPPORT

- Explore local programs that provide job training and skills development.
- Attend classes for GED preparation, financial skills, and parenting, often offered through churches.
- Look for support if you're re-entering the workforce after a difficult period.

FINAL THOUGHTS

YOUR JOURNEY ISN'T OVER

If you're reading this, let's have a real talk. You are still in the battle, and that's incredibly important. You have a unique story to share. You've faced tough times that felt unbearable, but you came out of them not just surviving, but stronger than ever.

Through every challenge you've faced, every setback that tried to bring you down, and every moment when you thought you couldn't go on, something greater was shaping your story. You are not just a survivor defined by your struggles. You are not just a number or a label that limits what you can achieve. You are not doomed to a life without hope. You are a shining example of strength and resilience. You are a fighter, actively working on your own personal growth. You are meant to spread positivity, even in the darkest times.

So, take everything you've experienced, the hard times, the victories, the lessons learned, and use them to drive you forward. Let your story inspire others who may need hope. And remember this important truth: You were saved for a reason.

To keep moving forward, to create, to guide others, and to love without conditions.

The road ahead may be long and full of obstacles, but you won't be walking it alone. Keep your chin up. Stay strong in your beliefs. And show up for yourself every single day. The most exciting parts of your life are still ahead of you, waiting to be written.

MY REAL TALK WITH GOD—WALKING OUT THE 12 STEPS

These aren't official words from Alcoholics Anonymous. These are my reflections, my grind, my prayers, and my lessons as I walked through the Steps in my own way. The 12 Steps gave me a structure, but God gave me freedom.

What follows is not a manual—it's my story of how I wrestled with each step, sometimes stumbled, but always found grace on the other side. These aren't just "steps" on a wall. They're the path that pulled me out the pit. If you're serious about change, walk these out one day at a time, with God leading the way.

1. **Admit the truth.** You're not in control. I was wrecked. Drinkin' had me twisted. I kept losin' battles I thought I could handle. The first step was getting' real: I couldn't fix me.

2. **Believe in somethin' bigger.** Not religion. I needed a Savior. I started believin' that God could clean me up when I couldn't.

3. **Surrender the wheel.** My way nearly killed me. I gave God full control. No more half-steppin'.

4. **Take inventory.** Write it all down. The hurt I caused, the pain I packed away, the choices I regret. No filter. Just truth.

5. **Confess it out loud.** I told God, told myself, and told somebody I trusted. Shame lost its grip when I spoke it.

6. **Prepare for the real work.** No more blamin'. No more hidin'. I was done with the old me.

7. **Ask for healin'.** All of it. I begged God to take away every toxic part of me—my pride, my anger, my guilt, my shame.

8. **Make your hit list**. Everyone I hurt— names that brought tears, some brought silence but I wrote them all.

9. **Make it right where you can.** I apologized when I could. Sometimes it was a phone call. Sometimes it was just forgiveness in my heart. No ego. Just humility.

10. **Keep checkin' your heart.** Slippin' back is easy. I learned to check myself daily. Admit mess quick. Stay accountable.

11. **Stay connected to God.** I prayed. I listened. I asked for strength, not just sobriety. It's not about bein' clean. It's about bein' close to the One who can save you.

12. **Give it away.** What God did for me wasn't just for me. Reach back. Mentor. Show up.

30-DAY

DEVOTIONAL

DAY 1

SCRIPTURE: ROMANS *5:8*

"But God shows His love for us in this: While we were still making mistakes, Christ died for us."

REFLECTION

God didn't wait for us to sort things out. He looked at our struggles, our mistakes, and our challenges and still called us His children. That's what true love looks like. If you think God loves you only when you're perfect, you've missed the point.

PRAYER

God, thank You for loving me even when I'm not easy to love. Help me to believe I deserve that love.

CHALLENGE

Today, stop feeling sorry for your past. Accept God's love as a gift you don't need to earn.

DAY 2

SCRIPTURE: 2 CORINTHIANS 5:17

"Anyone who is in Christ is a new person. The old life is gone; a new life has begun!"

REFLECTION

You are not the same person you once were. You might still feel like the old you, but God has made you new. Let everyone else talk about the past; you focus on your new life.

PRAYER

Lord, help me remember each day that I am a new creation. Help me embrace that truth.

CHALLENGE

Think of one part of your old self you want to let go of. Write it down and then throw it away or burn it. Let it go.

DAY 3

SCRIPTURE: PSALM 34:18

"The Lord is close to those who are brokenhearted and saves those whose spirits are crushed."

REFLECTION

You don't have to pretend to be fine. God is near to those who are hurting, not just those who act strong. Real strength is admitting, "God, I need your help."

PRAYER:

Father, don't let me hide my pain. Be with me in it and heal what I can't fix myself.

CHALLENGE

Talk to someone today and be honest about how you're feeling. You don't have to carry that burden alone.

DAY 4

SCRIPTURE: PROVERBS 3:5-6

"Trust in the Lord with all your heart and don't rely solely on your own understanding."

REFLECTION

Sometimes, your instincts might not align with God's plans. Trusting Him means letting go of the need to control everything. Allow Him to guide you, even when it doesn't make sense at times.

PRAYER

God, help me trust Your plans over my own, especially when it feels uncomfortable.

CHALLENGE

Before making any decision today, big or small, take a moment to pray about it.

DAY 5

SCRIPTURE: JOHN 8:36

"So if the Son sets you free, you will truly be free."

REFLECTION

If you've struggled with addiction, know that Jesus has freed you. Don't act like you're still stuck; that's not true freedom. Walk in the freedom He gives you.

PRAYER:

Jesus, remind me that I'm free from anything that held me back—my habits or my past.

CHALLENGE

Get rid of one thing today that tempts you to fall back into old habits.

DAY 6

SCRIPTURE: GALATIANS 6:9

"Let' s not get tired of doing good, for at the right time we will reap a reward if we don 't give up."

REFLECTION

Recovery isn't always exciting. Some days feel slow. But don't stop trying. Consistency matters, even if nobody else sees it.

PRAYER

God, give me strength when I'm tired and feel unnoticed. Keep me steady in my efforts.

CHALLENGE

Stick to your daily routine today.

Pray, work, and rest. Do what's right, even if it feels dull.

DAY 7

SCRIPTURE: JAMES 5:16

"Confess your sins to each other and pray for one another so that you may be healed."

REFLECTION

Healing comes when you stop hiding your struggles. Talk to someone who understands your journey. Honesty leads to freedom; secrets keep you stuck.

PRAYER

Lord, give me the courage to be real with someone I trust. Help me drop the facade.

CHALLENGE

Reach out to someone today. Go beyond surface-level conversation; talk about what really matters. You might help each other.

DAY 8

SCRIPTURE: ISAIAH 43:18–19

"Forget the past; don't dwell there. I am doing a new thing!"

REFLECTION

You can't move forward if you're always looking back. God is doing something fresh in your life. Don't let old regrets hold you back.

PRAYER

God, help me release my past so I can fully embrace what You're doing now.

CHALLENGE

Write a short letter to your younger self, then forgive that version of you for past mistakes.

DAY 9

SCRIPTURE: MATTHEW 5:6

*"Blessed are those who hunger and thirst
for righteousness, for they will be filled."*

REFLECTION

Instead of chasing after unhealthy highs, seek out God. Let the same passion that once led you to trouble now drive your faith.

PRAYER

Jesus, increase my desire for what truly matters. Fill the empty spaces in my heart with You.

CHALLENGE

Skip one bad habit today and replace it with something positive, like prayer, reading, or helping others.

DAY 10

SCRIPTURE: PHILIPPIANS 1:6

"He who began a good work in you will carry it to completion."

REFLECTION

You are a work in progress. Don't expect to be perfect. Focus on growth. God is still shaping you.

PRAYER

God, thank You for not giving up on me. Keep working in my life, even when I fall short.

CHALLENGE

Celebrate one small area where you've grown today, no matter how minor it seems.

DAY 11

SCRIPTURE: ROMANS 12:2

"Do not conform to the pattern of this world, but be transformed by the renewing of your mind."

REFLECTION

The world tries to mold you into something God never intended. Allow Him to change your thinking. Replace every lie you've believed with truth.

PRAYER

God, help me rethink things. I don't want to live like I did before. Show me a better way.

CHALLENGE

Write down three lies you used to believe, then declare God's truth over each of them.

DAY 12

SCRIPTURE: 2 CORINTHIANS 5:17

"If anyone is in Christ, the new creation has come: The old has gone, the new is here!"

REFLECTION

You are not defined by your past. What you've experienced doesn't determine who you are now. Your past is just one part of your journey, not the entire story.

PRAYER

Lord, remind me today that I am made new. Help me live my life reflecting that change.

CHALLENGE

Say this out loud to yourself: "I am not my past. I'm a new creation."

DAY 13

SCRIPTURE: PROVERBS 13:20

"Walk with the wise and become wise, for a companion of fools suffers harm."

REFLECTION

The people you spend time with matter. Being around the wrong crowd can take away your peace and time and even affect your freedom. Choose friends who support your goals and values.

PRAYER

God, give me the courage to distance myself from relationships that hold me back.

CHALLENGE

Think about the five people you spend the most time with. Are they helping you grow or pulling you down?

DAY 14

SCRIPTURE: PSALM 34:18

"The Lord is close to the brokenhearted and saves those who are crushed in spirit."

REFLECTION

You don't need to hide your pain from God. He understands and is there for you in your moments of sadness, anger, or hurt. You can bring all of those feelings to Him.

PRAYER

God, meet me in my difficult moments. Stay close when I feel broken.

CHALLENGE

Take 15 minutes of quiet time today, without distractions. Allow yourself to feel whatever you need to feel and invite God into that space.

DAY 15

SCRIPTURE: 1 CORINTHIANS 10:13

*"God is faithful; He will not let you be
tempted beyond what you can bear."*

REFLECTION

Temptation can be tough, but you are not powerless against it. God always provides a way to overcome challenges if you look for it.

PRAYER

Lord, help me notice the ways out when temptation arises. Give me the strength to choose wisely.

CHALLENGE

Identify your biggest triggers. Make a plan for how you'll respond when they come up next time.

DAY 16

SCRIPTURE: PSALM 1:2-3

"But those who find joy in the teachings of the Lord are like trees, planted by streams of water."

REFLECTION

If you want to grow, get rooted in God's Word. When you stay strong in your faith, you can weather life's challenges.

PRAYER

Dear God, help me appreciate Your Word. Let it bring strength from within me.

CHALLENGE

Take time to read one Psalm today. Afterwards, chat with God about what you read, like you're having a conversation with a friend.

DAY 17

SCRIPTURE: PROVERBS 4:23

"Above all, protect your heart, because what' s inside shapes everything you do."

REFLECTION

Not everyone deserves to influence your feelings or thoughts. Be mindful of what you allow in your life, whether it's music, chats, or habits. They can change who you are.

PRAYER

Lord, shield my heart from negative influences. Help me be wise in my choices.

CHALLENGE

Decide to remove one thing today that pulls you away from your values.

DAY 18

SCRIPTURE: MATTHEW 11:28

"Come to me, all of you who are tired and burdened, and I will give you rest."

REFLECTION

Taking a break isn't a sign of weakness; it's necessary for recovery. You don't have to constantly push yourself to prove your worth. Just rest in Jesus.

PRAYER

Jesus, I feel worn out. Help me find peace in You, not just collapse from exhaustion.

CHALLENGE

Take a genuine break today. Disconnect from your phone and stress, Just breathe and relax.

DAY 19

SCRIPTURE: HEBREWS 10:23

"Let us hold tightly to the hope we have, for God is faithful to keep His promises."

REFLECTION

When things don't go as planned, hold on to your hope. God hasn't abandoned you; He keeps His promises.

PRAYER

God, when doubts creep in, remind me that You never let me down.

CHALLENGE

Send a message to someone encouraging them with hope. Uplifting others will uplift you too.

DAY 20

SCRIPTURE: EPHESIANS 6:11

"Put on God' s armor so you can stand strong against challenges."

REFLECTION

Every day can feel like a battle in different ways. Make sure you're prepared. You're not alone in the fight.

PRAYER

God, help me wear Your armor today. Give me strength to stand firm.

CHALLENGE

Before you head out, say: "I'm not facing this alone. God is with" me.

DAY 21

SCRIPTURE: JOHN 15:5

"I am the vine; you are the branches.

Without me, you can do nothing."

REFLECTION

You don't have to handle life on your own. Stay connected to Jesus for your strength and guidance.

PRAYER

Jesus, help me remain close to You. I don't want to go through life by myself.

CHALLENGE

Start your day with a simple prayer before doing anything else, even before checking your phone.

DAY 22

SCRIPTURE: COLOSSIANS 3:13

"Forgive others as the Lord has forgiven you."

REFLECTION

Forgiveness doesn't mean forgetting or making excuses; it means freeing yourself from bitterness.

PRAYER

Lord, help me forgive those who hurt me, even when it's tough. I want peace instead of revenge.

CHALLENGE

Write down the name of someone you're upset with, and pray for them, even if it's hard.

DAY 23

SCRIPTURE: PSALM 119:105

"Your word is a guide showing me the next step."

REFLECTION

Sometimes life feels unclear. God's Word can guide you, even when you can't see the whole path.

PRAYER

God, illuminate my path. Show me where to step next.

CHALLENGE

Choose a Bible verse to carry with you today. Read it when you're feeling lost.

DAY 24

SCRIPTURE: JOSHUA 1:9

"Be strong and brave, for the Lord your God goes with you wherever you go."

REFLECTION

You've overcome many challenges. Remember how far you've come. You're stronger than you realize, and you're never alone

PRAYER

Lord, grant me strength. Remind me that You're with me, even in tough moments.

CHALLENGE

Face one small fear today. Show yourself that it doesn't control you.

DAY 25

SCRIPTURE: 1 PETER 5:7

"Cast all your worries on Him because He cares for you."

REFLECTION

Anxiety can sneak in. God wants you to let go of it, not carry it by yourself

PRAYER

God, I give You my worries. Help me find peace again.

CHALLENGE

Write down three concerns bothering you. Pray over each one, then let them go.

DAY 26

SCRIPTURE: PHILIPPIANS 4:13

"I can do all things through Christ who gives me strength."

REFLECTION

You're not facing challenges alone. God supports you through tough times.

PRAYER

Jesus, give me strength in my weaknesses. Help me rise today.

CHALLENGE

Repeat to yourself throughout the day: "I can do this. I'm not alone."

DAY 27

SCRIPTURE: LUKE 15:20

"But while he was still far away, his father saw him and felt compassion..."

REFLECTION

God is not waiting to punish you; He's ready to welcome you back with love. You're never too far gone to return.

PRAYER

Father, thank You for loving me despite my flaws. Help me come back to You.

CHALLENGE

Think of something you feel guilty about and then allow yourself to forgive your mistakes.

DAY 28

SCRIPTURE: ROMANS 8:1

"There is no blame for those who belong to Christ Jesus."

REFLECTION

Shame can make you feel unworthy or like you don't belong. But Jesus tells us we are free from that burden. You don't have to do anything to earn God's love – it's a gift you already have.

PRAYER

Jesus, help me quiet the voice of shame in my life. I choose to embrace freedom.

CHALLENGE

Whenever you have a negative thought today, replace it with a positive truth: "That's not who I am anymore."

DAY 29

SCRIPTURE: MICAH 6:8

"Do what is right, love kindness, and walk humbly with your God."

REFLECTION

Being a good person doesn't mean being loud or seeking attention. It's about acting with integrity, being kind to others, and staying humble.

PRAYER

God, keep me grounded. Help me show love to others just as You have loved me.

CHALLENGE

Do something nice today for someone who can't repay you.

DAY 30

SCRIPTURE: REVELATION 12:11

"They overcame through the sacrifice of
Jesus and the power of their story."

REFLECTION

Your experiences and story are important.
Don't be afraid to share what God has done
in your life. Your journey might inspire
someone who needs hope.

PRAYER

God, give me the courage to share my
story. May it help someone else find strength.

CHALLENGE

Share a part of your story with someone
today. Even a small piece might make a
difference in their life.

YOUR STORY
YOUR JOURNAL

_____

_____

_____

_____

_____

_____

_____

_____

_____

_____

_____

_____

_____

_____

_____

_____

_____

_____

_____

_____

_____

YOUR STORY

YOUR JOURNAL

_____

_____

_____

_____

_____

_____

_____

_____

_____

_____

_____

_____

_____

_____

_____

_____

_____

_____

_____

YOUR STORY

YOUR JOURNAL

_____

_____

_____

_____

_____

_____

_____

_____

_____

_____

_____

_____

_____

_____

_____

_____

_____

_____

_____

_____

YOUR STORY

YOUR JOURNAL

_____

_____

_____

_____

_____

_____

_____

_____

_____

_____

_____

_____

_____

_____

_____

_____

_____

_____

_____

_____

_____

YOUR STORY

YOUR JOURNAL

_____

_____

_____

_____

_____

_____

_____

_____

_____

_____

_____

_____

_____

_____

_____

_____

_____

_____

_____

_____

YOUR STORY
YOUR JOURNAL

_____

_____

_____

_____

_____

_____

_____

_____

_____

_____

_____

_____

_____

_____

_____

_____

_____

_____

_____

_____

_____

_____

_____

YOUR STORY
YOUR JOURNAL

_____

_____

_____

_____

_____

_____

_____

_____

_____

_____

_____

_____

_____

_____

_____

_____

_____

_____

_____

_____

_____

YOUR STORY
YOUR JOURNAL

_____

_____

_____

_____

_____

_____

_____

_____

_____

_____

_____

_____

_____

_____

_____

_____

_____

_____

_____

_____

YOUR STORY

YOUR JOURNAL

_____

_____

_____

_____

_____

_____

_____

_____

_____

_____

_____

_____

_____

_____

_____

_____

_____

_____

YOUR STORY
YOUR JOURNAL

_____

_____

_____

_____

_____

_____

_____

_____

_____

_____

_____

_____

_____

_____

_____

_____

_____

_____

_____

_____

YOUR STORY

YOUR JOURNAL

_____

_____

_____

_____

_____

_____

_____

_____

_____

_____

_____

_____

_____

_____

_____

_____

_____

_____

_____

_____

YOUR STORY
YOUR JOURNAL

_____

_____

_____

_____

_____

_____

_____

_____

_____

_____

_____

_____

_____

_____

_____

_____

_____

_____

_____

_____

_____

YOUR STORY

YOUR JOURNAL

_____

_____

_____

_____

_____

_____

_____

_____

_____

_____

_____

_____

_____

_____

_____

_____

_____

_____

_____

_____

_____

_____

YOUR STORY

YOUR JOURNAL

_____

_____

_____

_____

_____

_____

_____

_____

_____

_____

_____

_____

_____

_____

_____

_____

_____

_____

_____

_____

_____

YOUR STORY

YOUR JOURNAL

_____

_____

_____

_____

_____

_____

_____

_____

_____

_____

_____

_____

_____

_____

_____

_____

_____

_____

_____

YOUR STORY

YOUR JOURNAL

_____

_____

_____

_____

_____

_____

_____

_____

_____

_____

_____

_____

_____

_____

_____

_____

_____

_____

_____

_____

YOUR STORY

YOUR JOURNAL

_____

_____

_____

_____

_____

_____

_____

_____

_____

_____

_____

_____

_____

_____

_____

_____

_____

_____

YOUR STORY
YOUR JOURNAL

_____

_____

_____

_____

_____

_____

_____

_____

_____

_____

_____

_____

_____

_____

_____

_____

_____

_____

_____

_____

_____

YOUR STORY

YOUR JOURNAL

_____

_____

_____

_____

_____

_____

_____

_____

_____

_____

_____

_____

_____

_____

_____

_____

_____

_____

_____

_____

YOUR STORY

YOUR JOURNAL

_____

_____

_____

_____

_____

_____

_____

_____

_____

_____

_____

_____

_____

_____

_____

_____

_____

_____

_____

_____

_____

_____

ABOUT THE
AUTHOR

Derek Brown was born and raised on the west side of Rockford, Illinois—an environment that forged his grit, tested his faith, and ultimately fueled his transformation. Born on October 8, 1979, Derek is now 45 years old and living proof that broken beginnings do not have to define the ending.

After years of addiction, personal setbacks, and deep-rooted pain, Derek rebuilt his life through purpose, passion, and the power of God's grace.

Today, he serves in the pharmaceutical industry as a workplace culture strategist, helping organizations create environments grounded in trust, leadership, and personal growth.

Beyond his professional role, Derek is a proud sponsor in Alcoholics Anonymous, a life and leadership mentor, and a respected public speaker known for his raw honesty, street wisdom, and heartfelt motivation.

Whether delivering a keynote address or sitting beside someone in struggle, his mission remains the same: to guide others toward healing, hope, and direction.

Derek is the devoted husband of Cynequa Brown—his partner in life since 2012 and wife since 2023—and the proud father of two daughters: Jasmine (24) and D'Maia (11). Through his story, Derek reminds us that no matter how far-gone life may seem, redemption is always within reach, and hope is never lost.